THE JOURNEY HOME

The Personal Testimony of Barbara Marie Gargiulo

Catherine D'Angelo Meade

FOREWORD:
by Catherine D'Angelo Meade

Do you believe her? No one has ever directly asked me that question, but they have hinted at it. They hear me tell a very short version of how I know Barbara and why we are writing together, and I start to see that look, the sideways look that almost pities me for being gullible. I recognize it now. It actually helps me to notice how important it must be for me to be writing with her and how careful I must be to get it right. I know that Barbara's testimony of her near-death experience can sound like supernatural fantasy in the wrong hands. She knows that, too.

The Journey Home

Let me introduce you to the Barbara Marie Gargiulo that I have spent years getting to know. Because first impressions can make or break an introduction, I use caution as I paint the picture of what a face-to-face introduction might look like if you met Barbara for yourself.

Barbara is petite and attractive. She smiles often, and her eyes smile, too. She is loving, kind, very real, and she truly *feels* genuine and present in each moment. Her pretty face, has tiny little features that decorate her perfectly. She wears makeup, but never looks all done up. She has a bronze tan all summer that carries her through until the parts of the year when she and her husband can get away to someplace warmer to refresh it. Her blond hair is cut short and stylish. It reflects her outward personality in the way that it flips up and isn't turned under. Her hair is managed with styling gel to give it a cool lift instead of lying flat on her head.

She stands at a self-assured, but not haughty, 5'3" and has an adorable shape. She walks every day to stay healthy. She carefully chooses food for her family, preferring to home-cook most of her meals. She walks confidently, but not with an attitude. She is a New Yorker, but recognizes that she doesn't have to possess all of those New York girl qualities just because she lives on Long Island.

She dresses conservatively, but not matronly. She gravitates toward pastel colors, choosing light pink, salmon or aqua most of the

The Journey Home

time when she dresses. Her clothes are always pressed to perfection and never worn out or mismatched. She is exact in her appearance, matching her jewelry and her shoes with every outfit. I'm not the kind of girl who cares about all that, but I have never felt like Barbara has judged me. She chooses to make her appearance a priority, but not because she thinks we all *should*. She isn't stuck on social graces, though she has perfect manners.

Her home is immaculate. Her car is immaculate. She and her husband John both enjoy decorating and tending to their house and yard. It shows. They keep their home in a certain way, always presentable to company. It's very welcoming to walk into the Gargiulo home, their quiet neighborhood the perfect setting for their nest.

Since her return to her body after her near-death experience, Barbara is very serious about her relationship to God and is very committed to her duties within the various ministries in and out of her parish. She teaches Pre-Cana marriage preparation classes for new couples. She has taken overnight watches in the tiny chapel in our town to ensure that the days of 24-hour adoration go uninterrupted. She runs a ministry of discernment for those trying to choose their vocation. In fact, as is common for Barbara, usually those who are lost and confused in this area find *her*. She runs a weekly prayer meeting in the evenings in her home. She attends Mass daily and daily takes Communion. She taught religion classes when her children were small, but has been called to work with adults more in recent years. She has organized and held women's retreats at different locations. She has been an integral part of group trips to Israel, Rome, Greece, and Turkey. She is available after Mass on designated days each week, plus whenever God calls her, to pray with the sick for healing. She knows the power of the Holy Spirit. She believes in the laying on of hands, and prays in tongues when she is led to.

Besides regular involvement in ministry, she is devoted to interrupting those plans whenever someone needs prayer. She stopped working outside the home completely more than fifteen years ago, which means Barbara and John have been relying on God to provide through her husband's paycheck alone, not easy on Long Island. They've chosen instead to have her answer all calls to ministry work. It has become normal for Barbara to be contacted most every day to meet with someone who needs prayer for healing. She schedules in as many as she can. She travels to bedsides and hospitals. She prays with some people on the phone. She has accepted that she is called by the Lord to serve in this manner. She is obedient and seems tireless. She often works through the night when she should be sleeping, forfeiting her plans in service to God, continually learning the lesson that maybe she should stop planning altogether. Each day has new challenges in these ministries, especially feelings of being pulled in many directions. Barbara

The Journey Home

talks often of this and seems to be learning to move with the tide and allow God to move her as He will. This short ministry resume of sorts is only a glimpse at the tornado of action surrounding an average day in Barbara's life.

Barbara, an imperfect human like the rest of us, comes with her personal flaws as we all do, but I absolutely do believe her to be called by God to the ministries that now grace her life. I believe she has seen visions and dreamed dreams, that she has been given the gift of prophesy and healing, and has been divinely led to use her gifts to serve in all that she does, with all those put in her path. Like many others who have walked in ministry with her for years, I see Barbara as a visionary, a prophet, a servant of the Lord.

The Journey Home

From the onset of this project in 2008, in an effort to keep the writing clear of comparison and to keep my own thinking clear of bias, I didn't spend any time researching other accounts of near-death experience (NDE). Instead, I thought it would be best to allow Barbara's experience to be the only one that I had ever heard in its entirety. I didn't want to be influenced by anyone else's account so that in writing out her testimony I would choose only Barbara's descriptions, especially when reaching for explanations of difficult, hard-to-describe facets of her experience. I am very glad that this was the course that we took as a writing team. Even in the editing phase, keeping Barbara's authentic explanations has been my objective in retelling her testimony.

Now as the book is finally set to be released, and the writing and editing of Barbara's account is completed, I have started reading other accounts of NDE. *After* by Bruce Greyson, MD is one such volume that I've found to be packed with unbiased research (Greyson & Overdrive, 2021). Included in his research is the scientific, clear-minded scrutiny of the mystery of what NDE's actually are. Also included in Greyson's research are hundreds of participants that gave their brief, snapshot accounts over decades of study. The affirmations for me were staggering. The principle characteristics of each account were quite similar in many ways to what Barbara experienced on the other side.

Not only did I learn that Barbara's experience has the same pivotal attributes that classify other accounts into the NDE category of out-of-body experiences; I learned that she is not the only one who has had difficulty putting her account into words. It's been comforting to me as a writer to see that describing what happens after we die with the limits of human language is not a simple matter in any case with any of the subjects in the study, and it lets us off the hook a bit about how long it has taken this text to get into print.

Additionally, it's also been a wonder to discover how much more detailed Barbara's account is by comparison. The length of time that Barbara spent in the presence of the Lord and the intricacy of the many details she relays make her story stand out even among other near-death experiences. For this, I am grateful that the Lord gave us this much time to get it right.

When I met Barbara fifteen years ago, it had been seventeen years since her NDE. Her life had already changed dramatically. If it hadn't, she and I would never have met. In her eventual work as the head of a healing prayer team that met in and around a Catholic chapel near our home, she prayed with my husband in his battle with pancreatic cancer. When he passed in 2008, Barbara and I were called to begin writing her story together.

We foolishly believed that we could finish writing her account in one summer of intense writing, and looking at this tiny volume it's difficult to understand why that *isn't* exactly what happened. God doesn't always do what we ask or expect, though; His plans are better than ours anyway.

Here in your hand is the short volume that represents the isolated testimony of Barbara's near-death experience in her own voice. A second book that also includes the full account of Barbara's NDE is called *Fifteen Summers.* In that book, the scenes are set for three different occasions when Barbara repeated her testimony in person from start to finish in my hearing: at an in-home fellowship, at a women's breakfast, and on a women's retreat. In *Fifteen Summers,* readers meet the prayer team and peek into the reality of a prayer world like most may never know.

Fifteen Summers explains in greater detail the way that God called us both to write together and how our shared experiences have shed light on the divine purposes behind God sending her back and behind our meeting at all. As God blurred the lines of two very different Christian religious backgrounds, we cried and laughed, prayed and ministered, and become fast friends. Isn't God something?

The Journey Home

INTRODUCTION:

My name is Barbara Marie Gargiulo. I had a near-death experience on June 3, 1991. I died on an operating table during surgery, and I met with Jesus. He gave me messages for my own personal life and other messages to bring back here with me. This is my testimony.

It has taken many years to finish this book, more than I ever expected, and that's partly because trying to write it all down is like tainting the story. I feel like writing it almost cheapens it. First, I imagine readers won't understand it the way I tell it because I'm trying to use earthly words to describe the divine. I'm explaining an experience and a place that has no geographical location or sense of time. I'm trying to relay an intimate moment that wasn't just a moment. It was significant enough to change my life, my thinking, my heart, my ideas for my future, my perspective on every single thing. This isn't just a story, and it loses its value and importance and some of its special-ness when it gets into the written word, even the spoken word. All of the possible words feel inadequate. I write it down now because I feel like I have to. It's time.

Secondly, every time I share it, it's like a violation, stripping me of my own personal intimacy during an encounter with God, an encounter arranged for me personally *by* God. It's like sharing a moment that's as private as the intimacy in a marriage. I've said before when I have given my testimony in public that I feel like the encounter is stolen when I share

The Journey Home

it, and that the value of it is cheapened by trying to tell other people what happened. There are no words to explain the depth of the intensity of private moments between spouses. Imagining the true love of a married couple and then trying to explain what they see in each other's eyes or what private togetherness feels like may help people to understand what I mean. Who could explain those moments? The elements of moments like those are physical, emotional and spiritual all at once, and they're not easy to explain. That's sort of what I deal with when I attempt to share my testimony.

But, I need to speak up. I have to speak up because I encounter people today who don't even believe that there's a heaven and a hell, and too many that don't live life

The Journey Home

knowing there is a place that awaits them that is much greater than this. There was a time when I was very public, and I told this story to small prayer groups, large groups, in churches, on retreats or whenever I was asked, but that's not the way. This book is the way for the messages I received from God to get out there. I'm supposed to write this down.

What happened to me after I left my body on the operating table is beyond human words. Our language just doesn't have what I need to explain the extreme of the emotions or the beauty or the intensity of it. It's more than what we are able to experience here on earth, and we just don't have the vocabulary for it. In an oral telling of the story, I try to use *very, very, very* to get my point across, but even the redundancy of that sounds wrong, especially in writing. Re-telling it never seems to do it the proper justice.

Opening myself up to criticism has made it difficult to share my story and messages as well. Though I haven't encountered a majority of scoffers, there have been some who have not trusted that my testimony is real, and the heartache of not being believed is painful. God showed me in my prayers about this over the years that there are three ways in which people who hear this testimonial believe it and grow spiritually from it; none of them depend on me and how I tell it.

The first is through a shared experience. Those who have a similar experience of their own or have heard of someone who's been through a near-death experience are likely to believe and understand without difficulty.

Likewise, those who have a personal relationship with me know me to be honest and trustworthy. I'm grateful for those people in my life who have never questioned me because they know my character. They strengthen my ability to stand and tell my story again and again.

The third way that people come to know my testimony is true and accurate (and truly the only way) is that the Holy Spirit gives them the faith and grace and acceptance to believe it through their own private revelation. Though relationship and shared experience contribute to acceptance and belief, the only real way for us to accept anything is when the power of the Holy Spirit reveals the truth to us.

Knowing this takes the burden of the reader's acceptance off of me. Though I do hope and I pray to give a most accurate and detailed account here that will be beneficial to anyone who reads it, I further pray for Holy Spirit revelation for each reader.

The Journey Home

CHAPTER 1:

As I look backward through my formative years, my childhood, my teens, the early days of my marriage, I can see it. I can see how God was preparing me the whole time. With that in mind, I could start my testimony from way back in the beginning when I was just a girl journaling and praying on my own, but I'm not doing that. Though it might make sense to see how God put things together from the start, to see His plan in all of my days up until I died, I don't need to go back that far into the past to explain the events of June 3, 1991 and the ministries born from them. I couldn't tell all of it at once anyway. It's too much. I know now that all of the details of my life before my near-death experience had relevance, that it all had a pur-

The Journey Home

pose that connects with this testimony, but what's most important is relaying the messages that were given to me on that day to bring back with me, so I'm beginning instead by starting with the morning of the outpatient surgery where I died.

My husband John and I arrived early that morning at Syosset Hospital on Long Island in New York. It was around 5:30 am. I was scheduled as an outpatient having day surgery. The procedure was supposed to take between 15-20 minutes. It was a routine laparoscopic exploratory surgery of the abdomen and pelvic area. Including prep time and paperwork and recovery, I'd be in and out of the hospital in less than five hours. My husband John, of course, was with me in the prep room.

The Journey Home

Our first baby, Justin, by then five years old, had been born nine-and-a-half weeks early. Thankfully, he developed into a healthy child, but those early days of worry over his wellness weren't easy on our family. With our next baby, Jessica, I went into early labor at just twenty-four weeks. Though by then Jessica was a healthy toddler by that point, she had also had a difficult time when she was first born. This put any subsequent pregnancies of mine into the high-risk category. We had visited one obstetrician after another hoping that one of them would tell us we could have more children without these complications and early labors. That hope had been diminishing as we went from doctor to doctor. Each one agreed that the complications were not as isolated as we had hoped, but rather a condition that would likely increase with each pregnancy. They said that it could progress to the point of unhealthy babies or even still-born births.

We agreed to show up that morning at the hospital for this outpatient surgery of my abdomen in the hope that it would both relieve my symptoms and reveal simple endometrial tumors as the cause of the complications. We were hopeful that once the troublesome tumors were removed, we could continue family planning and expect healthy full-term pregnancies.

We were so focused on our hope for resolution to the pregnancy difficulties that we weren't prepared for any risks on that day.

The Journey Home

An RN came to check me in and finish last-minute paperwork. She had sheets of paper that needed to be signed before we could start. She said they were standard for someone having this type of surgery. She rustled through the papers while explaining that the doctors needed permission to remove any of the following, depending on what they found, and then she read through the list. The list included everything from the minor removal of endometrial tumors on my ovaries, uterus, intestines, bladder, or abdominal wall all the way to the extreme of a full hysterectomy and even removal of part of my intestines. I didn't expect that. Neither did John. I wanted to just follow her lead and sign on the dotted lines so they could continue to prepare me for the surgery and not hold up their schedule, but I knew we

The Journey Home

were not ready to agree to the possibility that I could wake up unable to have more children. We had two beautiful children already, but we both wanted a large family with five or six kids, and couldn't stand the idea of something putting an end to that dream.

The nurse with the handful of papers had to make it clear that the risks were there. And even though John and I wanted time before making such a big decision, she was waiting for signatures and couldn't give us that time. It seemed like she assumed that the risks had been previously discussed with my doctor, and John and I must've already talked it over. She was mistaken. For her, the clock was ticking. It was her job to make sure that the operating room schedule didn't get disrupted.

The Journey Home

John and I searched one another's faces looking for a quick decision, or even a look of doubt, reassurance. Nothing was said. So, I just started signing as she assured me. "This is just a formality. They have to cover everything just in case. Radical measures are not expected to be necessary. You should be in and out in 15 minutes, and everything will be fine."

The last line was the one that included the possibility of the removal of my intestines. Again, I looked to John. It was clear that he was concerned, too. Time didn't allow for discussion. I signed. The nurse stacked and re-stacked the pile of papers, smiled, and said the anesthesiologist would be right in to put me under. Five minutes. She left us with her repeated assurances that this was just a simple procedure.

She then left us alone. We certainly didn't have time to get into a no-more-children discussion. No point in that, so we said our quick good-byes.

"I'll see you on the other side in a few minutes", he said, meaning the other side of the OR where the recovery room was. They came in to wheel me away. Once inside and settled on the gurney, the anesthesiologist told me to count backwards from 10. The last thing I remember was sleepily saying "five."

CHAPTER 2:

I awoke and found myself standing in a black void. It was blacker than black and vast, huge, like there was no beginning and no end. There was space all around me in every direction, as if I were standing in the middle of the universe like you see in pictures. Nothingness. It was just empty of everything. I was extremely frightened. "Where am I?" I thought to myself, terrified and confused. Immediately, I felt prompted somehow (not forced, but given the option to make my own conscious decision) to look over to my left. When I did look toward that direction, I could see my left arm as I'd always seen it, but it didn't look right because I could see through it. There wasn't an arm there at all really. What I saw in its place was this

The Journey Home

beautiful, golden light in the shape of my arm and my hand and my fingers, and it was transparent. "Wow," I remember thinking. "Something is really wrong here. Oh, my God! Where am I?" I was filled with fear, lost in it and completely incapable of understanding. (Note: as I've grown in my faith, I've been convicted by the Holy Spirit not to use the phrase above, but the honest truth is that during the time of my life when I had this experience, these were the words I often used to both call out to God for answers when I was questioning and confused, and the words I used to show surprise and disbelief. For authenticity's sake, I have chosen not to delete the phrase, though I know it is offensive to our Lord and to many people of faith.)

The Journey Home

It's hard to explain how time moved for me during this experience because it didn't pass like time passes here on earth. It's hard to tell how much time passed or how much time lapsed from one thing to the next, but I am trying. For me, things seemed to happen instantaneously or immediately, overlapping in a way, so I use those words a lot to try to tell you what it felt like.

I can explain what happened next by saying that at that moment, *exactly at that same moment* that I was praying my questions to God in my head and feeling fearful about the changes in my arm, while I was looking over to my left something again prompted me to look more in that direction. Let me try to explain what I mean when I say I was *prompted* to look up to my left. I

The Journey Home

mean there was an urging, not an outward, audible or visible request, but something I couldn't possibly ignore. It was a choice, but not one I was willing to deny. When I looked, the only single thing I could see way, way, way far away from me in the darkness was a speck of white light in the middle of the black void, and the second that I looked at it, I became enclosed, wrapped, kind of enveloped in this tunnel. Once I made that choice to look, to notice the speck of light in the distance, the rest immediately spun into action. If I hadn't been prompted, I never would have seen the tunnel of prism light starting. Just the inkling of the idea to look with my eye slightly in the direction of the light is what started the movement. Then it was moving, forming itself spontaneously around me.

The Journey Home

At the same time as that, I also began to move within the tunnel — as I was wrapped in it. For a fraction of a second I could still see the vast void as the black outside while the tunnel formed around me. There were rings of light in it, of prisms, as if a white-layered wind were laying around me as if it were a tornado of light laying sideways. The light formed around it, and in seconds, I was within this moving tunnel, moving me like an escalator that I couldn't feel under my feet, like a people-mover in the airport, moving a zillion miles an hour. I didn't step into a tunnel. It formed around me as I stood, and I couldn't feel a floor underneath me.

When I looked back, (over my left shoulder again) I could see my body below me on the operating table. Again, everything was happening very quickly. It was all so quick. In that instant, I thought, "How is this possible that my body is down there and I am here?" And I saw my body, but that's all I noticed. I didn't linger and look to take in other details. I did notice three other people, presumably medical staff in the room with my body, but it was so very brief that I didn't take notice of who I saw or what was being said or done. I couldn't describe the people I saw at all. I was confused by seeing my body from above, so confused by it all, but in the next flash of a second, the operating room scene disappeared. I was back in the vast void while the spinning tunnel was still forming. Again, my soul was still crying out inside me, "Where am I?"

The Journey Home

The light swirled around me and moved me while inside the whirling tornado of circling lights. The swirls that would be wind if it were an earthly tornado were instead millions and millions of prisms of light., and every color of the prism was so clear, so crisp, so brilliant. Not one color shone brighter than the next, but all colors stood out individually, each with its own brilliance equal so that I could see each one. Then as my eye saw them all together, they shone into the brightest of brightest white lights. I could see each color as individually as I could see the white. Don't ask me how I could see it all that way. Even my vision seemed different, enhanced, more capable of seeing. I was mesmerized by that. I could not take it all in. I couldn't look at it enough. I couldn't get over the extraordinary brilliance of it and how much it pleased me to look at it.

Then music began. The song — I know I can't describe it well enough to be understood like I mean it to be. I have searched for something like it here on earth to demonstrate, to compare, but I have never found it. It was music like I had never, ever heard before. It was elegant and powerful. The music itself had life. I don't know how else to explain it, except to say that it sounded like truth or life, like it was alive. It had life in it in the same way that the prism lights in the tunnel had life. The singing itself had life in it, too. Everything had life.

Besides the music, I could hear choirs of voices singing praise in a way that was higher than what we can produce or understand here on earth. It was the sound of exuberant joy. It was like many voices, sounds, musical notes, everything that you can imagine music to be. It was lyric and angelic. There were words, but not recognizable words that I knew or needed to know. They were almost like a foreign language, but not an earthly one. All of the singing and praying was in one tongue rising up as perfect sound. I didn't think of this in the moment, but now I can relate it to how it feels to be at a concert in a huge stadium when thousands of people sing the chorus of a tune that's familiar to them as one loud voice, but magnified. It's like that, but more than can be imagined on earth. The singing and the music were all in unison. The sound and tunnel and prisms and feeling from it were all harmoniously unified with the light and moving toward it.

I really have never heard anything as beautiful. I am not over-stating it to say that that sound is absolutely unknown to our human ears here on earth. It was the most amazingly angelic, life-giving musical expression of love that I have ever heard, and I felt as if I had automatically become a part of all of it.

Every part of me was joined into union with the light, with the music, the singing of the song. Like the prisms that had all colors and more colors than I had known existed, somehow the music was also a blending of all sound, and it become one with me. It included me, enveloped me. I was feeling it and experiencing it with my entire being as one harmonious expression, and it all just kept moving upward and upward toward this white light, and moving me along with it in this brilliant, beyond brilliant, white light.

I became aware that I wasn't alone. I could sense that there was someone with me, sort of behind me and to the right, but I never looked to see who it was. We were both traveling in the tunnel together. As we moved along, the light and the music and the song all joined in the progressive movement, everything accelerating and intensifying, the light becoming even brighter. It kept increasing. This brilliant white light held me close in every way, in every part of me. I want to describe this right; it's like the light enveloped me, and it did this from that very first moment that I even thought to look up at it. This light wasn't just illumination or a glow. It contained peace and comfort like nothing even describable on earth. It felt like an embrace, a welcoming, and it filled me. The filling just continued to intensify and intensify and with it my joy and praise for it. I felt in harmony with all of it at once and wanted to be nearer and nearer to it.

I am repeating myself to say that time is difficult to define in this experience, but I know that if I don't say it again it will sound impossible the way I'm telling it. Everything happened simultaneously and it also felt like it lasted a long time. For example, while in the tunnel, from the very start, I was asking questions in my mind, to myself, but not just to me. Each one of those questions was instantly answered by the pres-

The Journey Home

ence of that being (someone, something, I didn't know who or what, I say it was a companion) that was behind me just over my shoulder, with me to my right. I never looked to see who it was because I didn't take my eyes off of the light, the prisms, the tunnel. I knew I was getting answers from a sort of companion or chaperone. And the answers were in my heart and mind, not out loud.

While I was in the tunnel, I also saw spiritual beings in the walls of lights on either side of me. I don't know who or what they were, but I felt like they were just *spiritual* beings because they no longer had flesh and bones, like me; I didn't have flesh and bones anymore either. What started out as a few of those beings when I first noticed them ended up to be what seemed

The Journey Home

like thousands. Some were lying down. Others were upright. They were in a quiet, sleepy state of awake, and they were stuck in between the prism-lighted levels of the tunnel. Worst of all, they were not moving toward the brilliant white light. I was passing them as I traveled along. There were so many of them! Some were male, some female, different faces, different colors of skin, different ages.

Immediately upon seeing the first ones I asked more questions (still in my mind, not with my voice). "Who are these people? Where are they from? Why aren't they moving, too? Why are they just staying there? How can they not move with us?" I was very disturbed that they weren't moving along with us. It made me feel sad, but I felt it very deeply. Then I became overwhelmed with sorrow, like really grief-stricken for them. I had a deep desire to stop moving toward the light without them. I wanted to help them, to reach out and grab them if I could and take them along with me, with us. It was unbearable to feel their pain, but there was nothing I could do to help. I was moving along. They weren't. I began to plead with that companion, whoever it was. "Can't we please stop? Can't we please help them? Can't they come with us? Please. I want to take them with us." I asked the questions without my voice, and without audible sound, all of the answers to my questions were given to me telepathically. "These souls are not able to move any further right now from where they are. They are sad. You see and feel their pain, and you want to know more about it, but *they* understand why they can't move right now. They know where they are and why they aren't able to move forward just yet. They haven't accepted it, but were given total divine acceptance of it and knowledge of why. Because it is."

When I explain this in person, I break down in tears at this point over the admission of a surprising truth: that the sorrow I felt then was so great that I wanted to stop there in the tunnel with those spiritual beings instead of continuing to move toward the light. In truth, I would have died a thousand deaths (meaning earthly deaths) in order to take just one of those souls with me. And I know that this sounds like an exaggeration and also a contradiction to say that I would be willing to stop going toward the light after I just explained the intensity of the longing to get there, but I would have done it if I could have. That's how intense the sorrow was that I felt for those spiritual beings stuck in the tunnel. The emotional pain of not bringing them with me was powerful.

Over the years of sharing my experiences, many have asked me if the tunnel is what the Catholic Church calls purgatory, but I can't say I heard that word specifically in this experience. I can only say that I did know in the moment that even the souls stuck in the tunnel walls were trying to get closer to the light, and they could not get there. And I could see that they drew comfort from their nearness to the light even though there was an understanding that they couldn't get closer yet.

The Journey Home

Their comfort came from the light itself and their forever-longing to draw closer to it, be fully united with it, and consumed by it. Yet, the Source of the brilliant white light ahead was still out of their reach.

CHAPTER 3:

Traveling faster, I continued toward the Source of the light, my companion still near me, but not visible; I was now completely consumed with the goal of getting closer to what was ahead, moving along without my will, but not against it. Actually, the opposite was true. Even though I was moving along by some unseen force, not walking or climbing up, but sort of gliding, I wanted desperately for it to move me in the direction I was going, just to be nearer to the light.

Before us in the distance, I could clearly see an image. The glimpse of His presence made me become prostrate, first on my knees and then fully flat out, face down. I couldn't just stand up in the presence of The Lord. I couldn't keep from lowering myself in reverence of His majesty. There before me was Jesus! He *was* the pure white light.

He was the Source of the light I had seen, the light that drew me in, the brilliance I had to get to. Jesus really is the Light of the world. The brilliance had been emanating from Him. I had reached my destination; I felt that I was home.

The radiance that came from Him was beyond what I could stand. I felt that I could not even look at Him because of my nothingness. There wasn't really a floor, but I was face down and low. Kneeling on the non-floor with my hands next to me and my face down on the top of His bare feet, I noticed one clean nail wound in each foot. His feet were glowing white in color and the nail wounds were actually beautiful. I could see holes in the top of His feet. I could see deep into them to reveal bluish-white flesh around them and a little red dot of dried up blood over the flesh.

In that moment, I felt that my own unworthiness was too great compared to His holiness, His purity, His indescribable majesty, the majesty that kept me prostrate. And even though I was consumed by the love and the peace and the knowledge in the light and in His presence, being this close also made me feel like I wanted to hide my unworthy self from Him. The feeling of unworthiness was intense. I was extremely unworthy. My smallness and my unworthiness were so great that I wanted to do nothing but hide. I kept

The Journey Home

trying to move to the left to get out of His presence. His presence was everything, but I wanted to shrink back from Him because I felt the immense weight of my own sin.

Telepathically, there was a long conversation between us where I continually worshiped and simultaneously begged to be removed from His Holy presence because my own sin was too much to bear in light of His goodness. It was a lamenting groan or cry that came from inside me, but without words. I kept begging in reparation for my sinfulness, and I do not use this choice of words lightly. When I say beg, I mean begging and pleading like I could never before have imagined. With all of me, in wave-like rounds, over and over and over again, I begged. The only thing interrupting my rounds of pleading were wave-like rounds of my own praise and adoration for Him. The praises were like none I'd ever sung or spoken before. More than that, the words of worship coming from me were unlike anything I'd heard anywhere else. My praise was spontaneous and instinctive. It was the only thing possible that could come out of me, and it was everything I felt should come from me. It felt right. It felt natural. It was all of me, all I could give. And yet it was nothing at all compared to the Greatness that was before me.

It seemed like a lot of time passed with me prostrate and begging while also worshiping. And, yes. The two things were happening at the same time. Again, I don't know how much time passed, and I don't know why everything seemed to overlap. At some point I realized that the Lord was now pleading with *me*. He was beckoning me over and over again to rise up and come before Him.

"How can anyone ever stand before You?" I questioned again and again, reasoning and trying to protest. After saying this in my mind, I felt an answer. Eventually, I began to arise before the Almighty. Once I rose up (and I'm not sure if I was able to get to a standing position or just kneel upright), I felt the power of His love like a complete embrace. And it wasn't just love, I felt peace, calm, comfort and His healing power all around me at once. The feeling that I was *home* was very strong. I felt like I had come to where I had yearned to be for all of the days of my life, and without even knowing it.

The Journey Home

It felt like I'd been longing for this forever and in that moment it was finally fulfilled. I had achieved my true purpose, the reason why I had ever been created. Everything suddenly made sense as I was given the understanding that to be back *home* with the Lord is to be whole again. This wholeness is a completeness that can never be obtained here on this earth. It is a clear knowledge and understanding of who we are, why we were created and where we all belong. It is the answer to every question about life and destiny and existence. And most of all in that moment I had the answer to the most basic of human questions: is there really a place to go after this life? I suddenly had an assurance about the answers, that there is a life after death, and it was all wrapped up in the unfathomable love of the

The Journey Home

Lord in whose presence I now remained.

And He truly is the beginning and the end. The feeling of being in His presence was everything.

CHAPTER 4:

The very next thing I remember was a thought about my husband and my children. I began to see glimpses, flashbacks of what felt like far-away moments and events in my life. They were like very, very old memories. I mean, I was seeing them with my eyes, but all of it was miles and miles away in the distance with a vast space between me and what I could see. There was a feeling like I had lived it all like a thousand years ago. I say a thousand because I cannot figure out how else to explain it. It was so far back in my past, as if it were forever and ever ago.

The Lord waved His arm in a way that demonstrated He was showing me more. I saw my house from above. We were hovering over it. There was no roof. I could see my children inside running around in circles. I could hear chatter, though not discernible words. My parents were there watching them, and everything was exactly how I had left it that morning.

I could feel their memory. I could almost relive the moments, but from a very far-off place. I had an awareness that there used to be an attachment to them, but I didn't have that same feeling of attachment anymore. The only attachment in the entire experience was with the Lord...in that place...in His Holy presence. The most extraordinary and most memorable facet of the experience, and I still keep this part with me to this very day, was the enormity of the love. I could feel a consuming love, like nothing I'd ever felt before. At the same time, I could still feel the intense love I had for each one of the people in my family, too. I know that I carried that love for them with me into this place, but it was different. I didn't yearn to be with them. I understood that they did not *belong* to me. It was a strange and harsh and extraordinary realization to me. Up until this point, they were my all, my whole life. My children and my husband were everything before this, but it changed then to an understanding that the people in my family were never mine to begin with. It wasn't like I didn't want to be with them again; it was just that now I had a different understanding about that, that they were individually, each one of them (like I was), on a personal journey, and it didn't have anything to do with me, *per se.* It was about their own relationships with God.

The Journey Home

I also remember a giant outpouring of gratitude to Him that I had ever been given the awesome opportunity to be with them at all, to be a mother to my children, and to be John's wife. As with every other emotion, the feeling of thankfulness was so very extreme. It was overflowing like an explosion of gratitude from my heart.

This part of my testimony makes me very emotional. Whenever I speak it out in person, even now, I'm overwhelmed to the point of tears because of the enormity of the love for my husband and children and how it may be perceived. It's hard for me as a human, a loving mom and a devoted wife to admit to the idea of not wanting to be united with my loved ones in favor of wanting to stay in the light and all that that light rep-

The Journey Home

resented: the love, peace, contentment of reaching my final destination. I explain it by saying that this kind of understanding only comes from a conversion like the one that Paul had on the Damascus road. A defining moment with God that brings revelation from Him is the only thing that can convert the heart to be able to understand how I could walk away from the cherished love of my husband and children. It is hard to admit this, but I wanted to stay *there* in the presence of something greater. It was a love and peace more powerful than anything that ever could be here on earth. Even though in the present moment it's hard for me to understand how the love for them was displaced by anything else, it is true that it was.

Next, while on my knees, I began to look ahead of me as a giant panoramic-like screen was shown to me. Jesus was to the right of me. He moved His hand and arm in a sprawling motion like He was presenting something He wanted to show me, and pictures opened up. Before me were three large movie-like screens, like a trifold mirror. I was kneeling before the first screen as the Lord Jesus was to my right, next to the third screen. It was as if someone had turned on a movie. On the first screen to my left I saw moments, events, and situations from my past, some positive, some negative. There was a pause at some of the moments, like I was re-living them, one by one. I felt great pain and sorrow about things that I had done or things that I had said. Not only was I watching a review of dif-

The Journey Home

ferent interactions I'd had in my life, hearing those conversations and seeing the body language, I also felt my own intentions in those moments, and I knew the thoughts behind my actions. It was all very clear and transparent as it was projected before me. I felt totally exposed. And I was ashamed.

I was allowed to live it over again and feel it — not with my mind intellectually, but with my soul. I was given the great opportunity to see the effects that my behavior, thoughts and expressions had had on my own soul in relation to truth and to holiness. This became unbearable for me. I never saw myself as a terrible person who had sinned to such a great degree, but I could see it now, and I started pleading and pleading in reparation for the things I had said or done or neglected to do and say. I suddenly understood the damaging effects that my thoughts and actions and expressions had had on my own soul. In this gut-wrenching pleading, I begged and begged the Lord to allow me to leave His holy presence. I don't mean to sound confusing when I say that; just before I said I was longing to be in His presence and felt like it fulfilled me more than anything in my life ever had before. I still felt that, too, but I now also felt low and unworthy to be anywhere near Him and His great love and holiness. He didn't allow me to hide, though. Instead, I was surprised to find that He then became my only comfort.

Just as I felt unable to endure watching the replay of my own actions any further, the second of the

The Journey Home

three screens began to light up as that first movie rolled on. This middle screen showed the same scenes as the first, only now they were seen in a new light. I was given the opportunity to re-live each moment through the mind, heart and soul of the person who had been affected. I was feeling the fullness of the emotions and pain that I caused. I was shown how these actions affected how other people acted next, after our interactions. Because of certain words that I had said or things that I had done someone did not move forward in their day or in their life in the way that they could have. And it was caused by me, by my actions, my attitude, my words. This was more painful than I can say. It was horrible. On the first screen I saw how my own actions affected me personally, how they affected my own soul, and next I saw how those same actions affected other people and their lives. I felt responsible, accountable, and remorseful. It was so very painful.

No amount of pleading could ever render an account for my wrongs. Never. Why hadn't I seen it before? Why hadn't I noticed any of this while living it? How could I have been this clueless? Oh, yeah. Then the truth hit me even harder. A lot of times I had known. I had heard that inner voice in me saying, 'No. Don't do that.' Or 'Don't say that.' Why hadn't I listened? Why hadn't I seen it before? I saw myself as an unspeakable wretch, the very filth of the earth, of all of creation. It was torturous to watch this review, especially from a perspective where I saw that I really could have done things differently. The awareness I had

The Journey Home

about the weight of my own sins was powerful. Sobbing again in reparation, I started pleading to be completely hidden, to leave, to be removed from His presence. I didn't want to be in the Lord's presence because of the shame of my sinfulness, like Adam and Eve hiding from God in the Garden after original sin, like Isaiah, who said, "Woe is me. I am a man of unclean lips." They felt unworthy to be in the presence of God. With that, I was at His feet again, and it seemed like I stayed agonizing in that feeling for a very long time.

Jesus did not stop giving out His love to me when I felt this way — just like with Adam and Eve — God continued to give them His love, but their sin kept themselves from Him. Just like them, I was in the full pres-

The Journey Home

ence of the light, and I could not bear to be in His presence because of an awareness of my sinfulness. I stayed near the Lord, anyway. I was impure in the presence of purity, but I wanted the comfort that could only come from being with Him.

CHAPTER 5:

Next, the third and last movie-like screen to the right began to project its images. As the scenes of my short, 29-year life passed once again before me, I noticed that this time I wasn't watching through my own eyes or the eyes of those I had affected, but now I was watching those same scenes through the eyes of our Father. What was revealed to me was how each of my actions had an effect on Him, positive or negative, in accordance with His original plan for the creation. I could not see the Father, but knew that He was up and to my right beyond where Jesus was now seated. I was able to see and feel the sorrow and the joy that gave way to my Father's heart as the scenes went flashing by. I found myself again pleading in reparation,

The Journey Home

ashamed and begging to be removed from Their presence. This time I was able to make up for my mis-deeds for one exceptional reason, because Jesus Himself was between the Father and me. He really was my Great Advocate. He pleaded and spoke on my behalf. My words were nothing but emptiness. His words, however, moved our Father's heart. I do not know the exact phrasing. I remember my pleas and my continued sobbing, and Jesus standing up for me. The actual words aren't what I think about when I remember. It's the feeling of this great relief that I had someone advocating for me, loving me enough to stand up for me before the Father, someone who Himself took my place and became the atonement for my sins. I never did see the Father, but behind

Jesus, the Father was there. I knew that for sure.

Next I remember a feeling of sort of waking up, or coming to, or recovering from passing out or being slain in the Spirit. In that awakening, I found that I had been kneeling before our Lord with my head on His knee. I had been sobbing and pleading in that position. He was gently stroking my head with His left hand and comforting me in a way that no other could. He really was my only comfort. He Himself was all mercy. He Himself contained all that is love. My crying continued as I was filled with gratitude, full of admiration, adoration, thanksgiving. My praises to Him came flooding out of me again — and I don't mean with audible sound. Everything was telepathic, internal, but surely my voice of praise was spontaneously shared. I began to understand at that moment, where I acknowledged my own wretched humanness in light of His comfort and forgiveness that it would take an eternity to be able to rightfully express all the praise and gratitude that is due Him, to feel the weight of my own sin in light of His mercy.

Behind Jesus, there was an understanding that God the Father was still behind Him. He wasn't visible to me, but I knew it in my spirit. I stayed in that state of humble gratitude for a long time. Then Jesus said, "Let me show you what has gained your entrance here."

Two more screens were placed before me for a long, intense review. The first was a scene from approximately 3-4 years prior. I watched as I was talking and praying to myself while on the telephone with my life-long friend Penni. On the screen I saw myself pacing back and forth in the kitchen and foyer area of my house while talking and listening and internally praying throughout the conversation. I was asking God to tell me how to help, what to say. I wanted to ease her pain. It was late at night, and she needed to talk to someone who understood. My kids were asleep, so I gave her my attention. She was quite upset. She was talking on and on about her life and about how much she missed Scott. Scott had been a boyfriend of Penni's who she had planned to marry. Tragically, he had been decapitated in an automobile accident, six or seven years before that phone call. She had moved out to California

The Journey Home

from New York several years earlier to try to start a new life. She had called me from there. I could feel her pain very deeply as I watched the screen and re-lived the experience. I saw the both of us absorbed in our phone conversation.

She went on explaining how she just couldn't seem to get over it, that it kept creeping up time and time again. She thought her life would never move on, that she'd never find another love. The call lasted several hours. I noticed that I had shown great compassion on her in that moment. I watched myself pacing along with a heartfelt sorrow for her.

As I watched us talking on the phone in that scene, a radiating light was going back up to the Father the whole time. I knew the radiating light

The Journey Home

that traveled up indicated He was pleased by my actions. I could not see God Himself, but I understood without a doubt that the light led to Him, and I felt the sincere happiness that it caused Him. Jesus was waving His arm and indicating God was behind Him and was pleased.

I was still confused about why. I couldn't understand what was so extraordinary about this one phone call. Jesus answered my questions. "See what has brought such great joy to my Father's heart?" The Lord showed me that when we are in communion with Him and when we desire to be with Him, it brings joy to God. Even though I didn't go out of my way to please God in that moment of my life, what He saw was goodness. Pure love and compassion pleases God. I asked repeated questions in my mind about how this tiny insignificant act could have such a tremendous and significant effect on the heart of God the Father, and then I just understood that it did. It just did. That was it. Finalized. Every good deed that we do or say in communion with God's love brings a brilliant joy and light to the Father. I was made to accept it as the truth that it is.

The second intense review screen showed a scene from my life from just two months prior. I recognized the scene right away when it started to unfold. It was a morning when my husband John and I were with the kids in our tiny church in Manorville. We were in the back on the left side during Sunday Mass. This was the day I had gone up to a woman at the front of the church that

The Journey Home

I didn't even know. I saw myself and remembered how the desire to go up to her had started out mild, but became stronger and stronger. Along with the desire to go to her came a powerful feeling of grief that washed over me. I felt true sorrow. I spoke to John at the end of Mass, all teary-eyed and impatient and wanting to go to her.

  I saw the conversation where I convinced a confused John that I had no choice but to walk over to her, a stranger that I felt I needed to console, even though I didn't even know why. And I had no plan for what I would say. I told John that all that mattered was getting to her to say I was sorry about her sadness, about her broken heart. I had to comfort her in some way. I saw myself push forward down the narrow aisle of the church, going in the opposite direction of the people exiting. As I got closer to her in the front of the church, I felt the heaviness of her grief increasing. I didn't speak at first. All I did was place my right hand on her left shoulder. As I did, I saw the replay of how my sincere prayers poured out from me to her. Once I had touched her, there was a release of that grief. After a period of quiet understanding between us just holding my hand upon her shoulder, I watched as I repeated, "I am so sorry about your loss and about your pain, your sorrow. I am so sorry about your loss and about your pain, your sorrow."

Though I didn't know it before this, that 75-year-old woman, whose heartache had become my own, who God had somehow prompted me to show compassion on, had suddenly lost her lifelong husband a week before while we were away in Florida. As the scene replayed this intimate and spontaneous moment of love, the Father's heart was beaming. As before, I was allowed to see the light of it, the fruit of it, the joy from the purity in the love pouring and flowing upward toward God the Father. I saw this pure white light, not the golden light, but pure white light that comes from pure love. I saw the heart of our Father beaming with great joy and delight. And though it was a joy to see, I didn't understand how that one moment mattered. It was just one moment. The phone call with Penni was also just one moment that demonstrated how I showed concern, but it was nothing special either. Any true friend would have done the same. These scenes were just tiny glimpses into moments of my life. Yet, Jesus said that these two actions could gain me entrance here? After first showing me 29 years of sinning He had now shown me what pleases God the Father and what brings Him joy — and it was two seemingly insignificant moments, not purposeful good deeds or acts of service or mission work. Listening to a grieving friend late at night on the phone, then reaching out to a sorrowful widow in compassion: these are the acts that brought joy to Our Father.

Over the years of repeating this testimony, I have been given a greater understanding. Those isolated acts of self-less love and compassion made a difference to the Lord because when we act in pure love, we are in 100% communion with the Father, with all of creation. God is love. But it's important to know how we get to that point of communion with God. It's only through Jesus. It's *only* through Jesus. I was given a chance to see how I twice acted in love, first toward a friend and next toward a stranger. God showed me how *through Him* and through *knowing Him* and acting in *His perfect love* I could carry that love and compassion in prayer to even a stranger. He enabled me to do that through His love. These two experiences showed me the heart of God, and that's because God Himself ministered to Penni and to the widow *through* me in those moments. And there's no glory in that for me. It was all God. We all have the ability to be the hands and feet of God when we are in complete communion with Him.

The Journey Home

CHAPTER 6:

After that, Jesus said, "Look." He pointed His index finger into the vast, black void. It was as if a huge window opened up beneath His finger, and I could see only a giant, darkened sea of water before me. I was just above it, looking down upon it. He said, "It's like this..." He took His index finger again and placed it into the middle of this black-like sea. The very instant He did this, the sea turned bright with golden light. Then another window opened up so that I could see a shape like the earth. It was very, very far away. We moved closer to it. As we moved closer, it took the color of the earth still spinning in a vast, black void. We came right upon it, meaning we were suddenly looking right over it like from a satellite or spaceship view, like hovering next to it, in front of it. He stood over the spinning earth as I watched. He placed His index finger upon what looked like a globe. I could see clearly; His finger was right over the area where I lived. Again, the instant He touched it, it lit up with this bright, golden light, starting out as a dot that moved in a straight line around the whole earth. It was almost like an equator line, that was a bright, golden light that circled the darker globe.

Another window now opened, and I was brought into my very recent past. I saw a scene of myself getting up out of bed in the morning. I didn't say a word to my husband John next to me. I washed my face. I went into the kitchen and started making breakfast and packed up my husband's lunch. The kids came in. They sat down to eat. I was kind of

The Journey Home

abruptly placing French toast slices on plates, pouring syrup, glasses of juice, etc. Everything was being put down on the table and the counters or plates, but it was being done hastily and with an attitude. I never talked, nor did they. I was allowed to see my facial expressions, thoughts, and theirs also. I felt saddened. It continued.

Next, I saw my husband off to work. Again, no words, just a hasty, wave-like motion. I was allowed to follow along as he drove to a deli around the block to get coffee on his way. He saw someone coming out of the deli. He nodded only, no greeting. No happy facial expression. That was unlike him. He always wears a very happy-go-lucky expression in public, but not this day. I watched as he paid at the counter. There was no

The Journey Home

usual, friendly morning conversation. Nothing. He proceeded to work, encountered his fellow-officers. Again, no usual friendly conversation took place there either. Next he encountered the inmates one-by-one at the jail where he worked. And I saw the trail of darkness that was left behind him. I briefly followed back and watched everyone that he had encountered, starting with the deli scene. I saw how a darkness came over each one of those people and then all of the people *they* encountered after that, every one of them now being surrounded by a cloud-like darkness. It traveled through and through down the line.

Next, my children were shown to me. My son Justin went off to pre-school. Both of my kids had been fighting on our way there in the car.

The Journey Home

Justin went in to the school. I saw him throughout his day there. He was not sharing with other children. He wasn't as cooperative or productive as usual. He looked sad and angry. While he was at school, Jess and I attended a playgroup with other stay-at-home moms and their kids. My daughter wasn't her usual joyful self either. Once again, following through, I saw the encounters of each of my children, and the black-like cloud that was passed on to each person with which they interacted. The darkness was passed from person to person in all of these scenes, and it had started with me. My vision of it began to pan out as I felt myself sort of backing up. I could now see it all from a distance as the darkness traveled until I was backed up enough that I was no longer able to see the people. Backward still to

The Journey Home

the continents, then back farther to the whole globe of the earth spinning in the void as when we first started.

I saw the bright, golden line of light that once had been around the globe being erased as that dark cloud-like-ness traveled from person to person. I saw it disappearing before my eyes until it was no more. The globe became dark all around. I was very saddened by this as I was made to understand that I was responsible for it. I was the cause of that ripple-effect spread of darkness.

Then He said, "Now see". At His very words, a new window opened to begin the same morning wake-up scene from my bedroom. Only, this time as the scene unfolded, I got out of bed joyfully. Though no words were spoken, I had a song

The Journey Home

in my heart. I washed my face as I greeted the morning. I approached the kitchen with all of the tasks I was about to begin with a skip in my step. I looked out the large bay windows into my beautiful, tranquil back yard, and I felt happy. It was filled with sunshine and I very consciously smiled at the new day. There was thanksgiving in my soul. There were hugs and smiles for all and a goodbye kiss for my husband. Each moment of each task was filled with love. There was love in my heart as I looked upon each one of them. As I sent each one off there was a beautiful golden light that traveled around them. Again, I followed my husband's next steps. This deli scene was completely the opposite from the first one I viewed. The pre-school and playgroup scenes were turned around, too as each person was encountered with joy, with peace, with charity. Every person in turn was a receiver of this bright and beautiful golden light, not a dark cloud. I was allowed to see it all unfold throughout their day at a close-up view. The scene then became further and further removed as we began to back away.

We traveled backward and upward until we were up high enough to see the chain of people starting from my own house. Each one was like a pinhead of a dot of golden light. They were joined with each person's light and together they formed a bright golden line of light that lit up a new circle around the whole globe to re-form the line of light like an equator. The dots of light created the line. I was filled with such joy and awe. I was amazed at what I was witnessing. I was in absolute astonishment how my small life played a part in the whole of it. It was overwhelming to me. I was especially amazed at how all of it could be this impacting without any words ever being spoken. Our actions and our emotions, our intentions, our attitude: that's what counts. I could never ever have imagined that one sole person could have such a tremendous impact, not just upon a few others, but upon the whole world. Nor had I understood that it could ever come from the simplicity of our everyday tasks and events.

Whenever I speak in public about this scene I remark how it makes me think of the familiar saying about 'getting up on the wrong side of the bed' and how much we need to remind ourselves not to shrug that off. We do need to pay attention to the very real consequences of not starting each day with love and light.

****

Next I was back to the large, black-like sea. We were looking down upon it. Once again, Jesus placed the tip of his index finger into the center of the body of water. At the moment of contact, the sea lit up like last time with a bright, golden light. This time I was allowed to stay for a moment and take a much closer look at it. The light that started out from the center as a drop began rippling outward. It had a wave-like effect upon the body of water. The golden light radiating out from the water became bright enough to light up the whole black void around us. I remember it so perfectly, so clearly to this day; it has had a lasting effect on me. The imagery serves to remind me that quite often all we say or do (the good and the bad) has a rippling effect upon others and upon the whole universe.

The Lord then began to minister to me personally about how much time in my life I had already wasted and how much peace I had forfeited by speaking harsh words. I don't know every detail of the scenes that were shown to me at that time. I remember bits and pieces. I remember flashes of sorrow, flashes of scenes that seemed to be given to me in the moment and aren't meant for me to dwell on, scenes of me and my husband arguing and yelling where I said things I shouldn't have said. I know it included the pain of what it did to our children who listened. The biggest personal sorrow that I came back to this earth with, one I still carry with me, is the difficulties I've had with miscommunications. The true knowledge of it is a lot to endure. That's my suffering.

This particular piece of my experience is very private regarding my accountability. The details of how the Lord was calling me to change are meant for my own reflective intimate time with the Lord, so I don't want to add more about it here. I can say that the sorrow I felt over this issue was intense, and I'm grateful that He didn't leave me in that place of ignorance about His will for my life to be better, for my behavior to change. It brought me to a new awareness of how I should be living.

CHAPTER 7:

After that last scene, I was given a time of rest to absorb it all. I was kneeling at the feet of Jesus, but I felt different this time; I felt as one with Him. I could feel the love of the Father and the place that Jesus has as Mediator. I stayed in that place of joy. After a review of my life with my mistakes and my triumphs alike, because of Jesus, I emerged with a feeling of satisfaction that I had pleased God, like a child might feel when their parents show approval.

I was allowed to rest in His peace and knowledge and joy and love. I felt pleased that I had served God. And as the years have ticked on, I've learned again and again that it's all about serving through the love of Jesus. It's not just the service; it's the love in the service. And the love is light. And they are God. Jesus is the Light of the world, the Light shining among us.

If we aren't serving with true love and joy, then it's just a minimal task. Serving French toast by throwing it on my son's breakfast plate, for example, isn't the same as a true act of charity and service. Our actions go out as nothing or they go out as pure light or as negativity. It's just like the equator line that lit up when Jesus touched it. In that first scene, God showed me the world was black and void until Jesus touched it and brought light. He physically put His finger on it and it made light appear. Without Him, without the love that He gives us to give out, we aren't serving Him, and our deeds are not in union with the light.

The Journey Home

I sat in this moment a long while. Time is so very different outside of these bodies so I can't tell how long it was. At some given point, I became aware that I had to go back. "Go back?! I don't understand". In that moment I really didn't expect to ever leave. I didn't know that I was going to have to leave. Here I was at the feet of Jesus; where else would I rather be? I pleaded, begged. I sobbed. The sobbing was out of my control, impulsive and intense. How could I ever leave this place? How will I ever leave His Presence? I did not understand at all how I would do it. I know I'm speaking in extremes when I say this, but I was in the most sorrowful state of disbelief. I felt as if I would die....let me re-phrase that....that is how it would have felt in earthly terms. What it would have been like in the spiritual form was much greater. The emotional distress and pain would be greater, I mean, because it's pure there without the flesh. The emotion is open and raw and without boundaries outside the body. This is why the pain was so great for those beings I passed on the tunnel along the way who weren't moving with me, with us. I hope I'm explaining it well when I say that every emotion (including the sorrow of knowing I must leave there) was magnified while out of my body because there were no barriers to stand in the way. All was in its fullness. The intensity of the emotion of it all is indescribable from inside our flesh. When my flesh was left behind, the purity of every emotion intensified exponentially.

I sobbed and sobbed at the feet of our Lord, pleading to not be taken from there. Imagining going back to my body, away from Him, was like a living hell to me. There isn't any greater sorrow for us for all eternity than to be separated from God. I think it's especially hard to come into the fullness of the presence of our Lord and then be turned away or removed from it. I tell you this as an absolute truth. Nothing on earth or in heaven will ever be more sorrowful than just that: the absence of His presence. That is the true meaning of death. That truly is the absence of life.

I was consoled only by the next visions that were shown to me then about my future. These included things that I had yet to accomplish. There was joy to wipe away some of the sorrow in that I was honored to have a future plan that pleased God, to be trusted by Him to accomplish things for His kingdom, and to be asked to serve Him, but there was no relief in knowing I had to go back.

There was a very long time of back and forth layers of communication with Jesus when He told me to rise from bowing at His feet. I was fighting with every possible thing I had to not come back to my body on earth, but His will must be done, and I couldn't help but see it. I had to accept the will of the Almighty against my own grave sorrow.

I don't remember every message that was conveyed to me next. I remember scattered statements, all of which consoled me about going back, all of them insights into my future. I don't believe I am meant to remember all of those details. I know that God gave me insight about what is planned for me, but I only remember them now one at a time, as each act of service is completed. Each time I accomplish one of these things, I have a *deja vu* feeling where I am back to my near-death experience and zooming toward the tunnel and speeding along to the moment where the Lord gives me a glimpse of a memory of that service revealed.

Then Jesus told me to tell everyone back on earth that He said, "It's so simple. *Love God with all your mind, heart, soul, strength* and *love your neighbor as yourself*," and it's the same message. Nothing has changed. It's simple.

Jesus waved His hand and arm again and one last window

The Journey Home

opened. I saw another black void like the universe and very far away, like a tennis ball size, I saw a spinning earth. The moment that window opened, I began to travel with Jesus super quickly and we were standing right over the globe. As we got closer to it, we were brought down and the vision narrowed and I was shown thousands and thousands of churches, all different steeples and denominations. "Look what they've done," He said while He started weeping. I was devastated to see the Lord weeping. I was troubled at Him being sad and disheartened, disappointed, and so very, very sad. I couldn't comprehend that Jesus was weeping. I knew that it was because of the division. He showed me a world where every church felt that they had it better, and right, but it was all divided. "They took the simplest concept from my Father. They changed it. It's simple. *Love God with all your mind, heart, soul, and strength* and *love your neighbor as yourself.*" I couldn't console Him in the way I desperately wanted to. I wanted to fix it. I knew that I could only have a part in consoling Him with my obedience, by telling people to keep it simple, by telling people to stop dividing.

I take that simple message to as many as I am able. I try to show people that God wants us to pass the faith on, that Jesus is our Redeemer, that we are accountable for our actions and that we need to *love God with all of our mind, heart, soul, and strength* and we need to *love our neighbors as ourselves* and stop complicating it. The division of denominations and sects of faith must stop. I believe that when it's authentically from God, these truths will be a part of it, and it will remain simple.

Finally, when giving way to acceptance, I was able to ask, "What is it that I must do to regain entrance back here?" I was prompted at that moment to look up. Jesus waved His hand in a sweeping motion; a beautiful window opened up. I saw my husband and my two children and many, many others, and I knew that I would have the opportunity to affect them.

At that, I heard these words in answer to my question as He handed me two golden keys to the kingdom. "You must pass on the faith to those who are entrusted to you." I understood then that Jesus meant for me to raise my children in the faith and to make sure that my husband didn't stray from his faith.

"That's it?" I asked telepathically. In my heart I heard His *yes* while He was smiling brilliantly.

Again, I began to question, "What do you mean? Just these three? What about all the others that you just showed me?" There were thousands in that vision He had been showing me where I would be ministering to many, many more people in my future. "I don't understand. How can it be so simple? How is it possible that that's all I have to do?" The questioning went on and on. I was assured that anyone that was added to the faith by my witness would be like a bonus, but not necessary in order to bring me back here to His Holy Presence. I remember that that was the only thing that finally gave me consolation. I thought, "Wow. That isn't so hard. I could do that. I'll be back here in a flash," I thought. Somehow, through all that immense sorrow, I thought, "This is going to be okay. I'll be back here, like tomorrow."

When I think about this in present day, I feel like this scene is similar to how the apostles stood staring at the sky after Jesus ascended into Heaven. They were waiting for His return as if it would be minutes-long, when in reality it has been thousands of years.

And though I have accepted God's will, I am still grieving the loss of not being there with Him, and I am still today waiting to get back home to Him. I imagine that my grief of being separated from God by coming back to my body is similar to the earthly loss of a spouse to death. I believe I understand the sorrow of a widow when I consider leaving the physical presence of God to come back here. I've counseled those in mourning. I hear them say that they feel like they can't breathe without their spouse, or they can't imagine how to live now that they're gone. That's how I felt at first, too.

The Journey Home

CHAPTER 8:

The very next thing I remember was being zipped back up into my body. I entered back in through the front chest area right about where my heart is, exactly the spot where we place our folded hands on our chest when we pray. I still shudder at the memory of the pain of that zipping up feeling. Putting on or getting back into my flesh was excruciating. The feeling of confinement is indescribable. Getting back into my own flesh again was physically, spiritually, emotionally and psychologically very, very painful. In a split second I saw the white walls of the operating room and then nothing.

When I awoke many hours later, I was in a hospital room looking at the cork of the bulletin board

The Journey Home

ahead of me, partially sitting up in a hospital bed by a window. John was there. I couldn't move. The pain in my body was unbelievable. I had tubes coming out of every part of me. I can't tell you what was worse: the pain that racked every inch of my body, or the reality of truly being back and stuck in my skin again. I couldn't process it all. I saw John sitting beside me. He looked frightened and exhausted and yet filled with joy that I had opened my eyes and was waking up. I could not speak because I had tubes up my nose and down my throat. There were a million things I wanted to say and yet I didn't really want to say anything at all. How could I ever express the tremendous pain I was in, or explain where I had been. I didn't know what went wrong with the surgery, either. I wondered what happened. John looked at me as if he wanted to say a million things, but just like me, he said nothing at all.

Our eyes met in that silence. I saw tears in his eyes. Tears formed in my eyes, too. It was one of those extraordinary moments in life where we get to learn that, in love, there truly is no need for words. There was just pure love between us right then, a heart-to-heart, soul-to-soul private moment for just the two of us. And it reminded me of how I felt in the presence of the Lord. The love, compassion, concern: all of it. We communicated all of that without saying anything. I felt the love from John, the silent communication with him, and it was just like when I asked a question in my mind in the presence of the Lord and the answers were given without spoken words.

The Journey Home

John and I have that same kind of connection. We have always had it. Right then, I recognized it as a gift from God that came from a true love. Ours was a relationship of true, undeniable, unexplainable, unspoken, but still communicated love, and it was especially obvious in that first waking moment after the surgery.

****

I didn't really know the details then, and honestly, we may never know all of what happened in that operating room, but essentially we found out later that during the operation the surgeons had inadvertently ruptured the membrane of my small intestine near my stomach while trying to view the abdomen with an electronic TROCAR surgical camera. The rupture caused me to bleed to death. We were never told the specifics of the life-saving measures used to bring me back, but John was told that I coded twice; one of the doctors even apologized, saying that he had messed up. Laparoscopic surgery turned into open surgery with two large criss-cross incisions made in my abdomen. We gathered from doctors that they called in a gastro specialist to operate that day and had had to take my insides out and put them back in. One report said they had taken 40 feet of my intestines out before replacing them. Doctors had to abandon the original intentions of the surgery because the rupture happened almost right away. No diagnosis about endometrial tumors or insight about why I had had two premature births was ever obtained. We did eventually get copies of some of the medical reports, but we still never felt that all of the information was in the records.

I couldn't leave the hospital right away because my intestines needed to heal. Doctors didn't want me to take in any food by mouth, even telling me not to swallow my own saliva, instead suctioning saliva into a small basin for days. I was hooked up to many different tubes and wires and instruments, one that pumped the bile from my system to avoid any digestion. The pain from the surgery, from the rupture, from the procedures and life-saving measures was compounded by that zipped up feeling.

I felt an excruciating pain at my spirit being pushed back into my body. There's no way to describe the amount of pain I felt at being zipped

The Journey Home

back into my flesh. Once back, I was feeling like a young baby might feel as his mom zips him into a snowsuit that's way too small, like I was confined, like I didn't fit inside of my body anymore. I felt the final zipping, the closure of getting stuffed into my flesh, with the final part of the zipper closing over my heart, and I remember screaming because it felt so filthy and horrible and disgusting to be back in it.

Besides all of that, the gas used during the surgery to inflate my abdominal cavity enough for the surgeon to see well, was working its way through my body and causing pain all over that I didn't understand. I felt as though I were dying, like God had only sent me back to earth to be in my body for a very short time. I believed that He was taking me back home to be with Him after this gift of a short goodbye with John. I really thought I would die soon.

The heartache of being back in my body and back to this life after having spent such a glorious private time with the Lord was just torture. I couldn't talk yet with the tubes everywhere, but I didn't have any words to explain what had happened to me yet anyway. I didn't know how to tell John or anyone where I'd been and what I'd experienced. It felt like a personal intimacy that I didn't want to forget about, but I also didn't want to share with anyone either. I kept the details of how I'd met with the Lord completely to myself.

It was traumatizing to have had this terrifying surgical experience, but it was also traumatizing to be back in my flesh again, magnified by the physical pain. Those early days were about my survival. I could see it on John's face, especially when I saw him weeping, that my life was still in danger.

****

The first mystical thing that happened to me upon waking was that I had a deep, unquenchable desire for the Eucharist, to take Communion. I kept writing it down on paper. Eucharist, Eucharist, Eucharist. The Eucharist, or the Lord's Supper, the actual body, blood, soul, and divinity of Jesus Christ present in the wafer of bread transformed at the Mass through the hands of an ordained priest, was all that I craved. The idea wouldn't leave me, and I wanted nothing else. Up until that

The Journey Home

point in my life of 29 years, I believed that the Communion ceremony was something done in remembrance of Christ's sacrifice on the cross. Even when attending Mass, I did it obediently as a ritual of my faith. I didn't understand the true significance of it. I never saw the Communion ceremony as a ritual of *inner* obedience. I learned through this that it is a true communion with the Lord. I had never had the fullness of that experience with the Eucharist before, even though I had participated in it through my own home parish every time I went to church.

I never craved Communion before. During Mass when the miracle of transubstantiation was happening, when the priest was taking a simple wafer and changing it into the actual body of Christ, I would pray

The Journey Home

quietly to myself hoping that God could hear me and hoping He would forgive me for my lack of belief. I'd pray that He would notice my dutiful obedience in taking Communion and help me to understand the mystery behind the tradition, but I awoke with a fresh, God-given understanding of this thing called Eucharist in that hospital bed. I don't have any explanation for how else my thinking could have been changed except through my encounter with Jesus. I can report this with certainty: the truth about the Eucharist wasn't found out through my own reasoning or through an intellectual process or through research. My thinking changed to exactly the opposite of what I had decided to think about the Communion ceremony for all of my days in church before this, even after religious instruction and years of practice. On this day, I was suddenly sure about the miracle of the Eucharist, and I was sure with all of me that the wafer was truly and miraculously transformed into the actual body of Christ. I knew the truth of the Eucharist, and that knowledge came with a yearning from deep within me to ingest it.

I also felt an uncontrollable need for a priest to come and bless me. Please understand; I never had such a thought before that day. I never had a desire or even an inkling ever before in my life to call for a priest to come see me. People who know me in my life now know that I am friendly with many priests. I have their private phone numbers. I have had them to my home for dinner, or call on them for support in many ways, but at this point in my life, I didn't have a close relationship with a priest. This wasn't a desire for a friend from the clergy to come sit by my sickbed.

It was the middle of the night now on the second day of my hospital stay, and I was sure I was going to die. I was in terrible pain. My chest hurt so much that I imagined I was having a heart attack. I physically felt horrible, and I felt my life was over. I could not breathe and I felt I could not die without the blessing of a priest. I began urging John to help me to get a priest. I still couldn't talk because of the tubes, but I was mouthing words, writing them and insisting to John with my gesturing that I needed a priest. He was very reluctant to get someone at that hour and tried to convince me that it could wait, but I kept insisting, kept bugging John and the hospital staff. I wasn't able to accept their refusal. "We will have to wait until morning, ma'am. We will call someone then." For me, it felt like life or death urgency. It had to be tended to right away. It was a very strong desire, much more urgent than I could convey. It was an entire body thing, an entire soul thing. It's not exaggerating to say that every part of me needed to see a priest. So, a priest was called in, and he prayed with me at 3 am.

Though I'd been begging for Eucharist and I'd expected the priest to administer last rites in anticipation of my pending death, neither of those things happened. Hospital staff had forbidden me to take anything in by mouth, including Communion. And upon a closer assessment of my condition, the priest was informed that last rites wouldn't be necessary. They were apparently hopeful that I would come through this difficult recovery with my life intact. He blessed me before he left.

Seven more days passed as I very slowly improved in the hospital. I had barely eaten at all yet, but medical personnel said that I was ready to leave for home. They removed the catheters and IV's and tubes a few hours before we left the hospital. I was scared to be discharged from the hospital while still feeling that sick. Though I was officially back in my body, I didn't feel like I was really back. After having such a life-changing experience with the Lord in another realm, in the spirit world, I was having a hard time accepting that it was over and I was expected to go back to life as usual. Nothing felt the same.

The Journey Home
CHAPTER 9:

On June 10th, seven days after my surgery, John drove me home. Home. I was a nervous wreck in the car about home. I thought of home as a good place to be nourished, to have healthy meals, and I wanted to eat, but I had only just had small meals of soft food on those last days before I was released. I had had tubes up my nose and in my throat. I was really nervous about taking in food at home. I was afraid that my body wouldn't be able to process it after such a trauma. I was also nervous about going home and not being able to take care of myself on my own, without the medical staff. "Oh, my God. I'll be on my own there, and I still can't go to the bathroom," I was thinking. I was full of fear. It was so long ago, but I remember that fear, that anxiety. It was truly traumatizing to be taken back home with all those worries.

I was also very confused about being back here. I mean, *here*, on earth, in my body. *Here*. I still felt out of place in my body, back in my flesh on earth. There was a lot of confusion for me, and it wasn't because of medications. I wasn't taking any medications that would cause that. I did not feel connected with the tangible, material world. It was sort of veiled.

I remember John being sentimental and very emotional about bringing me back home. He was really excited about it. We had gone over what must've happened in that operating room and how close I had come to never coming home. So,

The Journey Home

John was celebrating. He was just ecstatic that I was alive and giddy to finally bring me back to our house.

I can see myself right there on the front seat of our green Reliant K, pulling up to the house and thinking that I absolutely did not belong there. I know I had just been in the presence of God and it would be understandable to feel strange about calling this my home, but at that time, I didn't know why I felt removed from the familiar, and that caused a lot of personal confusion for me. The inner turmoil was unbelievable. I loved our house, our home, our family. I should have been as ecstatic as John was to be back home and to be alive and to be out of that horrendous situation in the hospital, but all I could think was that I didn't belong there, and I couldn't connect with my life. I just couldn't.

John tried to get me out of the car. I couldn't really move on my own. I was in pain everywhere. I had gone in for a simple procedure, but I wound up having major surgery, and I wasn't well yet.

I saw our front door and I didn't feel a connection to it. *That's our front door alright.* But, it felt like it wasn't really my home. I felt tortured inside by the disconnection. It seemed familiar, but it felt like something I was a part of a long, long, time ago.

I couldn't imagine how I would have the energy and stamina to get up the stairs of our front porch and how I would get into the house on

The Journey Home

my own two feet. John said, "Don't worry. I'm carrying you." When he carried me up the stairs, he made a joke, "This is because I didn't get to carry you across the threshold the first time, so I get to do it now." Then he asked, "Aren't you so glad to finally be home?" He had a big smile on his face expecting he knew my answer to be some kind of yes. His relief to have me home was obvious.

I did answer, "Yes," but then I added, "and no, not really." He heard me, but he didn't know what I meant. I wanted to explain to John right then that I had already been home, that being with Jesus felt like my true home. Instead, I said, "This isn't really my home. It's just a temporary house that I have been asked to be steward of." I didn't plan to say that. It just came out. I never wanted to

The Journey Home

hurt John, and it must've been hard for him to hear, but out it came anyway.

At that moment, there were a million things going through my head about the reality of what I'd just said. It was overwhelming for me to notice the truth of my real home with Jesus, and then have this beautiful house of mine feel secondary.

Looking at John's face and his excitement to have me home and alive, I could see he was in awe. He loved me. He missed having me in our home. He knew our children desperately wanted me back at home. The what if's that must've been on his mind about the other possible outcomes of that day were obvious. He always valued my life and our marriage and our home and

The Journey Home

our family, but maybe it all intensified on that day. My homecoming was a huge moment for him. He had been waiting for the last eight days to take me home from that hospital, worrying for my life. He had prayed for this moment where he could lay all that aside and thank God for answers to his prayers.

I also recognized that my life suddenly became more of a gift to me, and with that came responsibility and honor. And I wasn't feeling like God owed me any of it. Everything around me became an unwarranted blessing. I had been given this home with him and our family together as a gift. I was supposed to take care of everything and be a good steward of what I had. It was a huge responsibility. I was accountable. I had to take care of it. In one way, it was a burden and a weight; at the same time I also felt immense gratitude for the opportunity and the gift of all of it.

I felt all these things at once. When I was with the Lord, I felt every emotion all at once, and it wasn't overwhelming. It just happened. The surge of emotions that went through me at once while I was present with the Lord was just different from how we feel here on earth, not separated out or one at a time, but intensely overlapping. In this life, we can go from sorrow to getting a grip and moving on and maybe being set off again. It's not like that in the presence of the Lord, without our bodies. Yet, being back here on earth, I was still operating in that same way. I mean I was feeling gratitude and sorrow and confusion all at once, and powerfully. The power of the constant rush of extreme emotions was difficult for me.

To be back in my body and feeling everything so deeply was hard enough, but, I also had the notion that all of it, all of *life* here was very temporary. "You're just passing through here," I told myself. "It's just a fraction of a moment of eternity. If I live here for 100 years, it will just be the blink of an eye." Thoughts like these kept me detached. In my mind, there was no way to attach to people and things of this world again. I was sure I was headed back to our Lord. Jesus told me so. He didn't say when, but I assumed it was soon. With all of those thoughts came a rushing grief about feeling detached. "Who feels detached from their own body, life, and family? Oh, my God! I'm not attached to any of this." Intel-

The Journey Home

lectually, I tried to be rational and tell myself that this really was my house, my husband, my home, my children and my body. I should be attached to all of it. These are the thoughts that ran through my head in the 30 quick seconds on the way to our front door.

Laying in John's arms as he was reaching for the doorknob, I noticed the sadness on his face. I knew I had shocked him with what I had said. I had hurt him terribly to say that I wasn't happy to be home. If he'd known the details, he would've understood me, but I hadn't yet spoken to anyone about how I'd died and what I had seen while I was gone. There was joy and relief in me when we finally had the opportunity to really talk, when I could finally speak the whole truth, to finally let it out and share with my husband what

The Journey Home

had happened to me, but right then John didn't know why I would ever say something like that. He expected me to be as relieved and excited to be back home as he was to carry me in. I saw the effect that my words had on him, and I felt regret. I felt sorry.

And then I realized that I had just let out the first bit of it. "Oh, my God." I thought. "I just told John that something happened to me. How am I ever going to explain the whole story? He's never going to understand." I worried about how he would take it to find out I had discovered a greater love, something more intimate and something that feels more like home to me than what we shared. "How could I ever tell him all of that?" John is my partner, my spouse, my best friend and I share everything with him. I knew I'd have to find a way.

The Journey Home

John and I are soul mates, not in the way people throw around that term these days, but because we were truly brought together by a spiritual connection. Love and attraction and compatibility are not the only parts of our relationship. We had decided to get married because we feel a huge connection spiritually, physically and emotionally. Some women talk about their relationship to their husband and say, "He completes me," and they might mean that they aren't a whole person on their own and that being loved makes them feel complete. That's not how John and I feel, though. It's not why we decided to be together. We feel like we are *supposed* to be together, like it is meant to be. We don't *complete* each other; we are *meant* for each other. And it shows. It's obvious that we are in love. Ours was the only love that felt like this to me in my life…up until now. John didn't know that being with Jesus was even better, even more intense, more powerful and full of love than he and I could ever be. I planned to tell him, but I didn't know how or when yet. I was very worried about how he would react to learning the whole truth about what happened to me. Jealousy is real, and the Bible says that even God feels jealousy when we neglect our time with Him in favor of any other earthly thing. I was sure that John would be even more hurt to find out that I had felt a greater love than what we shared together in our marriage.

John wasn't feeling any of those things yet, though. He didn't know where I'd been and what I'd experienced. This was still all just the

The Journey Home

back-and-forth going on in my own mind. When I blurted out that this was not my home, I had rejected everything that our house represents. We had spent years making this house a home together, where family could gather and share love. The hurt on John's face said that he knew something had changed for me. He knew that I suddenly didn't feel the same way.

CHAPTER 10:

The kids were in the house with my parents waiting for us to arrive. I don't even know where they were exactly, if they were looking out the window or waiting at the door. I was so absorbed with what was going on for me personally, consumed with overlapping and intense emotions. I was spiritually changed and still feeling like I was on another plane of some kind. I was also still quite sick as my body recovered from surgical trauma.

What made me start crying when I came through the door was the intensity of the love there. In that moment I couldn't help but acknowledge the incredible responsibility of being asked to be steward of it. Had God really given me this great a responsibility, and so much love with which to accomplish it? I needed to love even more than I ever had before. These people and these things needed me to care for them, just like they had needed me before I went into the hospital, but now it was all so much more precious to me. Everything seemed fragile. The responsibility seemed much greater than before because now I also felt the responsibility to do it well. I had a sense of needing to take extreme care of it all, not just because of a daily chore or duty, but because of something much greater. I felt the responsibility of having to do all of this with more love than ever. Jesus had just shown me how important the love part is. Now I wanted to stay always aware of that. I now knew that every action, thought, and intention mattered. I knew I had to answer to God.

When I saw my father and my mother and my kids as I went through the door, the feeling of familiarity and the sense of ownership were missing. *My* kitchen floor, *my* wallpaper, even *my* kids: they all felt strangely separated from me. I was still overwhelmed with the love that came from being in the house, and I felt love in every interaction, in every part of our home, in every single thing, but none of these items or people belonged to me. The connection was missing. Nothing felt like it belonged to me, but it all felt like love.

Once settled inside, I tried to touch things to get them back, to bring me back. I wanted desperately

The Journey Home

to connect with what I had been close to before. I touched things, like a set of keys, and there was gravity and weight to them and a knowledge of what they were used for and what I knew about them, but they were just very different. I was not fully back in the physical, tangible world. I was still stuck in the spiritual.

I felt there was no connection to the chair where I was sitting. When I stepped on the floor, I felt the floor wasn't connecting to my feet. I had literally lost touch with everything earthly, everything that used to be real to me. We may not even realize throughout life how much thought goes into each object our eyes and hands encounter during a day, but when that ability to make connections was missing for me, I felt a complete separation from being back here at all, as if the connections to our personal things and to people are what keeps us here in this physical world in the first place. Where I'd been when I left my body was much more real than any other thing here on earth could *ever* be — and the knowledge of that left me weepy and overwhelmed to be away from it now.

Trying to reconnect to my life on earth felt like an adult trying to remember their entire fifth year of life. They could probably remember glimpses, days in kindergarten, maybe Christmas or their first day of school or their birthday party, but it would be hard to piece it all together. It would be distant. That's how I felt. I felt like I was very detached from the house, the belongings in it, and even the people in it, not just distant memories, but fragmented ones.

I had been a devoted wife and mom. We were a strong family with loving connections to each other. I had always felt more closely connected to them than to anything else, or to anyone else. I wasn't married to my work or in love with success or power or riches. John and I had created this home to raise our family. This is what we were together dedicated to. How did it happen that I felt like it was now so different?

There was a separation between the spiritual and physical worlds and I was stuck in the middle. In the light of the knowledge that I now had about eternity and truth and heaven and the presence of God, after the experiences I had, my attachment to every single thing here on this earth diminished exponentially. I felt like I had moved on. And that made me feel badly. It made me feel like less of a mother and wife and daughter and even homeowner. And that didn't make sense after feeling as though they were mine up until now. Explaining that to John would not be easy. Explaining it here in this book is not easy either.

Through it all, I could sense strong feelings from everywhere. Love was the strongest of those feelings. It was the first thing that I felt at all that was any sort of reminder of how I felt during my life here. Even though I couldn't connect with things, I could definitely feel love, that same love I had experienced in the tunnel. As soon as I came through the front door, the love started to flow. Even looking at John as he carried me, I felt love. Love rose above and pushed away the thoughts, the guilt, the confusion. And the love and devotion that had been there was even greater than it had been before. The feeling made me cry with the power of it.

Nighttime was hard once I was back home. For all of us, nighttime was hard. The routine of bedtime, the rituals that I had established for my children, were hard to just slip back into. I was used to putting my kids to bed with stories every night, but I couldn't connect to even that.

Visitors noticed, and when they asked me what was wrong, seeing a change in me and assuming maybe I was having some kind of breakdown, I answered by saying, "You have no idea how much I love you and how much God loves us." I didn't just say that one time; I said it over and over again when people asked me how I was doing. It was impossible to focus on the things of this world when I was now hyper-aware of the assurance of the spiritual realm. I couldn't explain how bright the love and the light are with God. I couldn't explain the peace. I couldn't contain it in my flesh; it's too big for our human bodies. Leaving the flesh for that short time brought me to a full knowledge of love and peace, and I couldn't just let it all go and return to business as usual as if it hadn't happened.

The Journey Home

CHAPTER 11:

I did eventually find my way back to feeling somewhat at home in my broken body again. I stopped living on the mountain top talking with Jesus and became grounded again, but not right away. My family members took turns staying with me for the first four or five days at home. My mom and dad, my siblings, my in-laws all cared for my children, and my home, and they cared for me as well.

Everyone could see that I was still not fully present. I saw and felt the love in everyone's actions, their intentions, their faces, their presence, and that love was more magnified than ever before, but it still felt like the people of my life were from very far back in my past, and everything else was remaining detached from me.

I know they had been discussing whether I was having an emotional breakdown because all I did was cry over the great amount of love that God has for us and has for them. I was constantly saying and repeating it with joy and amazement. I learned later that the consensus of the family was that I had had an intense spiritual experience. Maybe they just figured that because I'd had a brush with death, I was having an existential crisis. It would've been easier if I had been able to explain it, but I really couldn't do that yet. It was too soon.

On one of those early days at home, maybe on the 4th or 5th day, I asked John and my sister-in-law Lorraine to let me just go outside for a while. I wanted to sit on a lawn chair in our backyard alone. I imagined I would pray. I needed to feel at one with nature. I could talk to God about what had happened. I wanted to be alone with Him, in that place of communion. I wanted to sit with Him and ask why I felt everything so deeply still, and why I couldn't get back in my body even though I already was. I wanted to be back in my routine, to stop crying. Prayer with God had been non-stop when I got back, and it had been rendering me unable to hold conversations with others. I was still caught in the radiance and light and enveloped in it here on earth, even though it was in a lesser way. I didn't see visions of God or Jesus, but I talked with Christ in prayer constantly. I was really trying to get back to my life for those 4-

5 days, but I was stuck. The light around me hadn't yet ceased, and though I never did anything like this before, I knew I needed to spend time just sitting in nature with Him alone in prayer.

My intent in going outside that day was to sit in nature with the all-powerful Creator and see my own place in it. I had a hard time being contained in a house even. It was confining even further than just being stuck in my body, so I went out to nature to feel better. I wanted to get it straight with God. "Am I going back to You? Or am I staying here? If I'm here, I want to be grounded again."

John and Lorraine helped me to get situated outside in a perfect spot in the backyard facing the house, soaking in the warm sun and feeling some peace. As I sat there in prayer and communion with the Lord (for hours I think), I was sure that soon I would die. I felt I was just back in my body temporarily. I assumed that the reason I wasn't connecting to everyone was because I was about to die again. I thought I was only back here so that I could say a final goodbye to my family. I was sure about this because I hadn't been able to talk to anyone about it yet.

    I couldn't talk about what happened outside of my body at all. It felt like speaking up would be breaking communion with God, and I didn't want to do that. Being back here was hard enough, but losing that feeling of communion, that telepathic constant conversation with Him was just another level of separation that I didn't want to risk losing. I prayed earnest prayers to God about the confusion. I asked Him why I was back in my body, begged God to just let me go back home to Him again or to end this feeling of detachment from where I was.

As I sat and stared and prayed alone, I started to notice the natural world around me in the same way I had seen things in the presence of the Lord during my near-death experience. From right there in my own back yard, I could hear a roaring of the universe, almost like the ocean, but magnified and louder and harmonious with all of nature. When I looked down at the lawn by my feet, I noticed how little glimmers of light caught on each blade of grass, and it wasn't just light. The light became the prism light from the

The Journey Home

tunnel. I saw full rainbow prisms. When I looked around I saw this on everything, every leaf on every tree, on every flower, and the light from the sun in the sky was brilliant and magnificent. And everything moved rhythmically in a unified wave or dance of worship to God. And I could hear it all. I felt God speaking to me throughout as I prayed and I thought I knew what was happening. I focused most of all on the grass and how it swayed in unified worship to God, where every single solitary blade of grass was moving in sync. I was now more sure than before that I was dying again. I was expecting to move toward the tunnel at any moment. The roaring had such authority. That's hard to explain, but I knew that the sound had dominion and authority over all of the universe, over all understanding. It was powerful, but not frightening. It felt like a focused clarity on the truth that every living thing comes from that power and authority. With every leaf and blade of grass bowing rhythmically in worship, I sat still in a synchronized symphony of creation. And I sat there for a long time, and I became a part of it.

Family kept coming out to check on me. It was really late, now nearing dinner time. I didn't know I'd been out that long. I had lost track of time. I noticed them watching me quietly from the top of the stairs from the upper deck off my back door, then urging me to come back inside, but I put my hand up in silent refusal, saying no. I wasn't ready to leave the experience. I wanted to stay there taking my place with creation in quiet worship to God. I shook my head to punctuate my refusal. When John and Lorraine came out to insist that I come back inside, I slowly moved my gaze to them and saw them in golden light. I could see through their golden skin in the same way I saw through my own arm when I was about to enter the tunnel.

The peace and the love that were there for me while in communion with the Lord and with all of creation brought me a powerful sense that everything was one. I wanted that feeling to continue, but it didn't. The intensity of this day was isolated and extreme and the feelings waned from then on out. I understood that I needed to get back to my life, to go back in the house and get back to the world.

The Journey Home

As I was walking into the house, the experience was fading. By the time I got in, the roaring and the music of nature and creation had stopped completely. John and Lorraine were trying to get me engaged in caring for the kids while setting the table for dinner. Just moments earlier, I had been able to see through their arms; now they were trying to transition me into mealtime with the kids. I tried to be obedient to it, but I was talking with God even while trying to get utensils from the drawer. I looked at the contents of the drawer, but couldn't relate to them. I was praying in my head to the Lord and telling Him I was frightened and confused about whether I would ever feel connected again, whether I would die and not stay here at all. The difficulty in attempting to process the transition was intense. I was in-between.

Lorraine and John knew that I couldn't connect or care for myself and my kids yet, but a day or two later, John had to go back to work and Lorraine was heading back to Florida. I was *still* feeling disconnected, even from my children while they were trying to hug me. I was going through the motions. I was walking it out, but I wasn't in it.

I remember a day right around that time when I was trying to get dressed after finishing breakfast. I was standing in my room, going through my clothes, sliding hangers on the closet pole, touching shirts and pants and dresses, but having zero connection to them. Feeling the frustration with my situation, I cried

The Journey Home

out loud talking to God by myself in my closet and saying all of the things with my voice that I'd been praying in my head. "I'm begging You, God. You have to let me come back here fully, or let me go back home to You. If You brought me back here, why am I not *back here*?" And instantaneously, I felt a sudden change, and I was back.

I was unaware, but, Lorraine was standing in the eaves of my bedroom doorway. She saw me. She heard my prayer. I turned to see her in tears. Immediately, I worried that Lorraine would think that I had lost control. I said, "You just don't understand what happened to me. I'm not having a nervous breakdown. This is about the love of God, and how much He loves you and how much He loves me."

The Journey Home

She was crying when she answered, "I know. And John knows," she said. "We know that something major spiritually happened to you. We know it's not a nervous breakdown."

I nodded my head, also in tears. "Yes, but I can't talk about it yet. Just know that God loves you. I keep telling you that you have no idea how much God loves us and how much I love you." I was back, but my repetitions continued.

****

With John already back to work by the end of that first week, life slowly started to get back to its old routine, my body still in recovery. I'm actually still recovering in some ways after all these years. At times I'm sure that my body will never be the same.

Even though normalcy was returning, I hadn't yet found a way to tell anyone what had happened to me. I was searching for how to first share it all with John. While I was waiting for God to give me the words or the grace to speak to him about what happened to me, God spoke to John through a messenger in a dream instead.

John woke me up from a sound sleep in the middle of the night to excitedly tell me that he had seen an angel. John said he was told that I had something to tell him, and he was instructed to believe everything he was about to hear from me as the absolute truth. In his dream or vision, John said that the Archangel Gabriel was present (and he was absolutely *huge),* and he was accompanied by St. Joseph. Together they told him not to be afraid. They said, "Everything that happened to your wife was of God." In the vision or dream they handed him a key that signified the specific gift of acceptance. He woke me up to tell me what happened to *him*, but then urged me to finally tell him everything about what had happened to *me* while at the hospital.

That very night, as I started to share the details with him, I felt the expected pangs of heartache. I explained how powerful the love of God is, how intimate the time in His presence had been. God finally gave me the words to explain it. "I don't love you less; I love God more," I said.

And I felt peace about that. And there was no convincing necessary. John said he had known all along that something traumatic, but spiritual and mystical had happened. He said that everyone knew that *something* had happened and he wasn't surprised to finally hear the details. His receptivity and acceptance weren't just gifts to him; they were gifts to me, too.

****

When I died on that operating table, I was brought to a place of connecting our tangible, physical world with the spiritual one we often ignore. I was given understanding that every single thing that we say and do has weight. Every single action is significant. Every act, every word we speak, every sentence is important. When I was with Jesus, I could feel the emotional reasons for everything, good or evil, selfish or in love. It's true that every action is done with a choice. We have a choice. And Jesus showed me that we have to answer for all of it. That's what matters. That's the message I'm sent to deliver. Yes, we have Jesus as our Advocate, as our Savior, but we *will* all face judgment also, and these thoughts, words, and actions are what we will be judged on in the end. I was given full knowledge of all of that when I was there, but I couldn't get it out into words when I first came back.

When I first got back, everywhere I went, I could feel the weight of people's actions, feel the love or the absence of it, feel the pain or the peace in every act, every conversation, every glance. I had a new understanding as a gift from God. He gave me a heightened level of awareness and compassion and knowledge of other people's pain: physical pain and emotional pain. I could connect to their feelings while on an elevator or on a grocery line. Knee pain, breathing issues, whatever were absorbed by me, by my body when those in discomfort were near me.

I have been back here in my body for too long. I'm starting to forget. I used to walk around and talk about this all of the time. I cried and wept and felt upset all the time with extreme compassion for people around me — all the time. I guess I couldn't stay in that state. I had to go to work, had to care for my children, and to go on living.

The Journey Home

Through years in healing ministry, I have noticed that I do still have tremendous empathy for others, but it was much more intense in those early days.

The feelings here on earth may fade with time, but I will never forget the details of this experience or the impact it has had on my life, the way that I felt in the presence of the Lord, the things the Lord shared with me about what truly matters, about what moves God's heart. Everyone's actions have weight and an effect. Every action is significant. I cried for many months about it all when I first saw the truth of what really matters, and while it was that fresh I couldn't just put it out of my mind. And it made me cry. The notion that every place is Heaven overwhelmed me! *Thy kingdom come.* I look at dandelions for example, and I think of Heaven and God. The purpose of every single thing here is to magnify God and to glorify Him. I'm hoping this story will help people to see that. I was asked by God to explain His love and to share the accountability. We are accountable to Him for what we have done in this life. When we go home, we are accountable.

In my first 29 years, I thought that I knew God and loved God and even served God, but I also sinned against Him when my words and actions and attitudes weren't pleasing to Him. And I wasn't repentant. I hadn't acknowledged my behavior needed changing or asked God to forgive me, and I hadn't gone to confession since I was thirteen years old.

The Journey Home

Our behavior while we live here on this earth matters. We will all endure judgment. Even though we have an Advocate who loves us, who has saved us by grace when we believe in Him and repent, we will all still feel the sting of the life review: the judgement of our actions and our words and our attitudes.

Jesus is the Way to the Father. *No one comes to the Father but by Him.* Heaven is all about the Father. I was given the knowledge while resting my head on Jesus' lap that I cannot get to the Father without Jesus. Jesus first showed me my sins, then He wiped them out. He is the only Way to God. Because of the two examples of good deeds that Jesus showed me, I pleased Jesus. I believe that I was shown the many, many sins committed in my 29 year life before I met Him so that I might know my own unworthiness without Christ. And I was shown His amazing grace because it is true that the greater the sin, the greater His mercy. The sick need a doctor more than the healthy. He showed me my many sins and only two good deeds and it balanced. In other words, my good deeds which are not equal to my wrongdoing were acceptable to God the Father because of Jesus standing up for me. I could never get to God, could not cross over without going through Jesus, even though my good deeds were pleasing to Him. The deeds could not atone for my sins. They showed the Lord my own contrite and changed heart, the love within those deeds pleased God. I believe that when I acted in love, it was a reflection of Jesus in my life.

The Journey Home

Overall, the message for me personally and for me to bring back to share with others is that our actions do matter, that our life will be reviewed with Jesus, that we must know Jesus as our Savior and Advocate, but also that we must live well.

Experiencing the love of Jesus present in the light was truly an indescribable joy for me that gave me an understanding of how all of us are supposed to live. We cannot in our human flesh understand God and the power and might of His infinite love and wisdom and peace, and we cannot in our feeble and filthy sinful bodies understand even a fraction of how much grace He gives us in dying on the cross as a sacrifice for us, but when humans catch a glimpse of life outside of these bodies, when we truly can commune with God, become one with the song of all creation, we cannot help but long for it for all of our days.

I believe the Eucharist is the closest our human bodies can possibly get to knowing God — when we are ingesting the body and blood of Christ after the miracle of transubstantiation in the Mass. Even though the power of God is veiled in the bread and in the wine, this veiled way of communing with God is necessary while we are still in our flesh. We could never withstand the full, unveiled power of God from our bodies here on earth. And our human minds could never fully understand it. The Eucharist is a gift of holy communion.

Since I came back in 1991, I have lived differently. I am devoted to

The Journey Home

my faith. I am a daily communicant. I am a servant of the Lord in many ministries, but most of all, I am committed to spending time with the Lord in prayer alone or with others in many venues throughout the course of every one of my days. I have seen miracles in healing prayer and in circumstances of those around me that are far too numerous to count. This experience ignited my faith and I have been blessed by a second-chance life that has ignited faith in others along the way. I have dreamed spiritual dreams; I have seen miraculous visions; I have lived a mystical life since my return to my body. The anecdotes could fill many, many more pages. I live in the full knowledge that our God has absolutely no boundaries, that He is one hundred percent good, that His Word is truth, that He wants us to be in continual relationship with Him, and that He has prepared a place for us to join Him when we leave these earthly bodies. I know without any doubt at all that we are more than what our human eyes and hearts and minds and bodies can fathom.

When I first had this experience with death and with the presence of God I called it my *journey home*. I didn't know there was a term called *near-death experience*, and I imagined I was the only one who had been permitted to get this close to the Lord. Since then, I've heard some details about others who have had these types of experiences. Some say they went into Heaven. Some say they saw loved ones. Some say they saw pearly gates and streets of gold, but none of those elements were present when I left my body. I believe that I couldn't go into Heaven and only remained outside of it through my experience because I hadn't yet atoned for my sins. I understand the incredible privilege that's been given to anyone who has spent an intimate time with the Lord like I have, and I am grateful. Though I look forward to living my life and I am thankful for the time God gave me to return here and live with my family, I am also looking forward to what awaits me in death, looking forward to the day that I can return to Him, the only true Source of *home*.

About the author:

Catherine D'Angelo Meade, a teacher since 1991, is a dedicated mother to seven wonderful children in her blended family, and grandmother to two little sweeties so far. She is a writer, a musician, a leader, a lover of God and all things natural. She holds a BA in English, an MA in Linguistics, NYS teaching certificates in elementary N-6, English 7-12, and TESOL K-12. She became a Doctor of Education (EdD) specializing in English Language Learning in 2022. She has thus far completed half of a school building leadership certificate as well. She is currently working as an adjunct professor in her local community college. She shares a home on Long Island in New York with her adoring husband, Tom, her children, her parents, a dog, two cats, and eleven chickens. She can usually be found barefoot and singing while searching for a morsel of chocolate.

www.catherinedangelomeade.com
Instagram @catherinedangelomeade

Made in the USA
Columbia, SC
12 November 2024